THE PERSIAN VEGAN *Cookbook*

Raheleh Sarbaziha MD
Razieh Rosie Ganjeyha
Farideh Dadgostar

I would like to dedicate this book to my mom, Razieh. Thank you for cooking fresh and healthy meals for us every single day while working a full-time job.

I love you & I love your food.

Raheleh Sarbaziha

Contents

Rosie grew up in Qazvin, Iran and she has been cooking homemade meals since she was able to walk and help her mother, grandmother, and sisters in the kitchen. She can cook almost any dish from scratch and memory. The culinary art comes second nature to Rosie and her biggest passion is ensuring she and her family are always fed healthy, home-cooked meals.

Razieh Rosie Ganjeyha

Farideh, born and raised in Iran developed a passion for cooking shortly after she married in the early 90s. The social and cultural norms of that generation obligated new brides to cook for their husbands. She presently resides in Canada and her talent for cooking Persian dishes has grown just as much as she has. Farideh now owns and operates "White Rose Catering" - a gourmet catering company that specializes in Persian dishes.

Farideh Dadgostar

Raheleh Sarbaziha

The desire to create this cookbook came as a result of our modern times. As I have grown and become more aware, I have realized the significant importance of a plant-based diet for social, health, and environmental reasons. I have refined and "veganized" all of my favorite Persian dishes not only for the purpose of enjoyment but also out of sheer necessity. This is our vegan take on ancient cuisine. I hope you too will enjoy it and share it with your loved ones!

Dolmeh

SERVES 4 | PREP TIME 60 MIN

Items you need

1 cup of white Basmati rice
1 jar of grape leaves

1/2 cup of split peas (dried)
1 medium yellow onion, minced
1/2 bunch of fresh mint
1/2 bunch of fresh tarragon

1/2 bunch of chopped parsley
1/2 bunch of coriander
1/2 bunch of fresh cilantro

1/2 bunch of fresh dill
1 fresh lemon
1 bunch of green onions

1 tbsp of ground organic turmeric
1 ounce of fresh chopped ginger
2 tbsps of chopped mint

1 tbsp of organic tomato paste
4 Roma tomatoes, diced
1 tbsp of extra-virgin olive oil
Salt and pepper to taste

Directions

Boil 3 cups of water, then add 1/2 cup of split peas for 15 to 20 minutes and stir a few times. Drain the water in a strainer and set aside.

Soak the rice with warm water and 1 tablespoon of salt for 2 hours. Drain through a strainer, place it in a large rice pot with 3 cups of water, and bring it to a boil. Simmer on low for 10 minutes.

Drain the cooked rice and add it to the pot of split peas. Next, add 1 teaspoon of salt, 1 teaspoon of turmeric, and 1 teaspoon of ground pepper. Mix and set aside.

In a separate pot, fry and add 1 tablespoon of extra virgin olive oil and 1/2 of the yellow onion, garlic, and ginger, stirring continuously on medium-high heat until golden brown. Add all of the herbs and continue to stir for about 4 minutes on medium heat until they are soft. Once the herbs have softened, take that pot off of the stove and mix the ingredients into the pot containing the rice and peas.

Heat up the tomato paste separately for 4 minutes on medium heat. Add salt and pepper to taste, stirring the tomato paste into the large pot with all the ingredients. Squeeze half of a fresh lemon into the mixture.

Take a grape leaf and stuff with the rice mixture. In a separate pot, add the rest of the ginger and onions with 1 tablespoon of extra virgin olive oil. Repeat with the remaining grape leaves.

The sauce: purée the 4 tomatoes and squeeze a full lemon into the purée. Mix a tiny bit of salt and pepper to taste. Place the stuffed grape leaves into the pot and drizzle the tomato sauce on top. Let it cook on low heat for 1 hour with the lid covered. Cool down, serve, and enjoy!

Agheh Anar

SERVES 8 | PREP TIME 60 MIN

Anar means pomegranate in Farsi, and what's not to love about pomegranates? They are an incredible source of antioxidants, adding anti-aging, anti-cancer, and anti-inflammatory properties to this recipe.

Items you need

1/2 cup of extra virgin olive oil

1/2 cup of yellow split peas

1 cup of pomegranate juice (freshly squeezed preferred)

4 tbsps of pomegranate molasses

1 cup of jasmine rice (wash x2)

1 large white onion, minced

1 raw beet, grated

1 bunch of parsley

1 bunch of coriander

1 bunch of green onion

1 bunch of spinach

1/2 bunch of dill

1/2 bunch of fresh mint

Directions

In a large pot, add 4 tablespoons of extra virgin olive oil, onions, garlic, and ginger with a pinch of salt.

Fry mixture until golden brown. Add split peas into a pot along with 2 liters of water and 1 teaspoon of salt.

Boil the rice in a pot of water with a pinch of salt for 10 minutes.

Once the rice is prepared, take the rice with the water and transfer it to the other pot containing the peas, onions, etc. Cook on medium heat. Add the grated beets, chopped herbs, pomegranate juice, and 2 tablespoons of pomegranate sauce to the pot.

Stir on medium heat for 20 minutes, then leave on low heat for 40 minutes.

Serve and enjoy!

Khoreghteh Bademjan

SERVES 4-6 | PREP TIME OVERNIGHT

I have many memories of making this dish, yet I still manage to butcher the name. It can be served as an appetizer or a main course, depending on how hungry you are!

Items you need

1 large white onion, minced

2 large eggplants

6 garlic cloves, minced

1/2 cup of extra virgin olive oil

1/2 cup of split peas

2 tsps of cinnamon

1 tbsp of tomato paste

4 Roma tomatoes, cut into thick slices

1/2 cup of hot water

1 tsp of ginger, minced

1 lemon

Salt and pepper to taste

Directions

Peel eggplants the night before and season with salt.

In a pan, sauté the onion, ginger, and garlic with extra virgin olive oil until golden brown. Next, add 1/2 cup of split peas, 1 tablespoon spoon of tomato paste, and 1/2 cup of hot water. Add 2 teaspoons of cinnamon and stir frequently. Cover with a lid on low heat and cook for 40 minutes. Stir every 10 minutes.

Cut eggplants into small halves and place them into a frying pan. With a generous amount of extra virgin olive oil, cook until golden and soft. Take off of heat and set aside.

After 40 minutes, add the eggplant into the split pea stew. Then, add a few of the sliced tomatoes on top and cover it with a lid. Cook on medium heat for 45 minutes to 1 hour.

Squeeze the lemon juice into the stew 40 minutes into cooking and stir. Serve and enjoy!

Bademjan Shekampour

SERVES 4-6 | PREP TIME 60 MIN

Items you need

1/2 cup of extra virgin olive oil

1 large white onion, minced

6 garlic cloves, minced

1 ounce of freshly chopped ginger

3 Italian eggplants

4-5 tbsps of pomegranate molasses

1/2 cup of ground walnuts (fresh)

1 tsp of ground organic turmeric

1/2 bunch each of mint, parsley, and coriander

Salt & pepper to taste

Directions

Peel eggplants in stripes and leave some of the peel. Cut a slit to open the eggplant.

Fry onions, garlic, and ginger with 1 tablespoon of extra virgin olive oil on medium-high heat until golden brown. Fry the eggplant on a frying pan with extra virgin olive oil for 5 minutes on medium heat. Then remove and set aside.

Add half a bunch of chopped parsley, coriander, and 2 tablespoons of chopped mint to the onions, garlic, and ginger.

Mix in 3 tablespoons of pomegranate molasses, 1/2 cup of ground walnuts, 1 teaspoon of salt, 1 teaspoon of pepper, and 1 teaspoon of turmeric.

Fry mixture in a pan on medium-high heat for 5 to 10 minutes until everything is mixed and cooked.

Stuff the eggplant with the walnut and herb mix. There will be a tiny bit of the mixture left that you should leave on the pan.

Add 1/2 cup of water and 2 tablespoons of pomegranate molasses to the remaining mixture.

Place the eggplant back onto the pan and cook it in the sauce for 10 to 15 minutes on medium heat.

After 15 minutes, place the lid on the pan and cook on medium-low heat for 10 min. Serve and enjoy!

Khoreshteh Loobia

SERVES 4-6 | PREP TIME 60 MIN

This is one of my favorite dishes and can typically be found in the center of every Persian dinner table. The recipe was passed down to me by my mother, but I love being able to add my own twist to it.

Items you need

1 pound of string beans trimmed and cut into 1 inch pieces

1 carrot, diced

3 potatoes, diced

1 onion, minced

4 garlic cloves, minced

1 tsp of freshly chopped ginger

1 tsp of organic ground turmeric

1 tbsp of tomato paste

4 Roma tomatoes, diced

2 tbsps of extra virgin olive oil

Salt & pepper to taste

Directions

Mix chopped onions, garlic, and ginger into a frying pan with 2 tablespoons of extra virgin olive oil and cook until golden brown.

Add string beans, carrots, potatoes, and tomatoes. Stir and cook on medium heat for 5 minutes.

Add in 1/2 cup of water, 1 teaspoon of turmeric, salt, and pepper to taste, and 1 teaspoon of tomato paste.

Place the lid on the pot and cook for 45 min on medium heat. Serve and enjoy!

Baghali Polo

SERVES 6-8 | PREP TIME 120 MIN

Out of all the Persian rice dishes, this one has always stood out to me because of the fava beans. Fava beans are incredibly nutritious and an excellent source of fiber, manganese, and several other micronutrients.

Items you need

2 lbs of fava beans (frozen)

4 cups of basmati rice

2 1/2 bunches of dill

1 tbsp of turmeric

Saffron (a pinch)

Salt & pepper to taste

Directions

Wash the rice and drain (repeat 4 to 5 times). Allow the rice to soak with water and 4 tablespoons of salt for 2 hours.

In a separate bowl, add the fava beans and season with 1 tablespoon of salt, 1 tablespoon of black pepper, and 1 tablespoon of turmeric.

Use a food processor to chop up the dill or chop finely.

Drain the rice into a large strainer. Place the rice in a large pot and add 6 cups of water. Allow the pot to boil on high heat for 30 min. Next, turn off the water and drain the rice back into the strainer.

In a large pot, boil 2 liters of water and then mix the 2 lbs of fava beans with 1 tablespoon turmeric, salt, and pepper. Allow to boil on medium to high heat for 30 minutes or until the beans are soft. Then strain the beans.

Mix the dill with the cooked rice, add the fava beans mixture, layering them carefully in a new pot and place it on high heat for 16 minutes. Next, turn down the heat to medium for 45 min with the lid on.

Serve and enjoy!

Adas Polo

SERVES 6 | PREP TIME 120 MIN

This is the perfect dish to cook when you are craving rice but want a variety of flavors to tickle your palate at the same time. Pair this dish with a side of Persian cucumber yogurt, and you won't regret it!

Items you need

1/2 lb of Persian dates

1/2 lb of Persian raisins

1/2 cup of extra virgin olive oil

3 cups of green lentils

1/2 tbsp of ground turmeric

Saffron (a pinch)

1/2 tbsp of black ground pepper

4 cups of basmati rice

Salt & pepper to taste

Directions

Soak rice with 5 cups of water and 4 tablespoons of salt for 2 hours.

To prepare your saffron water, grind a pinch of saffron in a spice grinder. Boil 1 cup of water and mix with saffron, then set aside.

Place green lentils in a large pot with 6 cups of water. Add in 1 tablespoon of salt, 1/2 tablespoon of black ground pepper, and 1/2 tablespoon of ground turmeric. Cook for 20 to 25 minutes on medium heat. Then strain the lentils.

In a separate pot, fry raisins with extra virgin olive oil and 1/4 cup of saffron water. Then place aside when warm and soft.

Fry chopped dates with extra virgin olive oil and saffron water, then place aside when warm and soft.

Strain the rice and add it to a large pot with 6 cups of water and boil it on high heat for 20 minutes or until the rice is soft.

Take the cooked rice and layer it with the cooked lentils.

Add extra virgin olive oil to the bottom of a large rice pot, and then layer the rice first. In small layers, add the rice and lentils. Cook on high heat for 15 minutes, and then switch to medium heat for 45 minutes with the lid on.

Serve and enjoy!

Loobia Polo

SERVES 6-8 | PREP TIME 60 MIN

This is by far one of my favorite dishes. The veggies and rice combination is so satisfying. This simple and easy to make comfort dish has gorgeously developed rich flavors.

Items you need

4 cups of basmati rice

4 tbsps of extra virgin olive oil

1 large white onion, minced

3 lbs of green beans, cut in 1 inch

4 garlic cloves, minced

2 large portobello mushrooms, diced

4-5 tbsps of organic tomato paste

2 tsps of cinnamon

1 tsp of ginger, minced

Directions

Soak rice with 4 tablespoons of salt and 6 cups of water for 2 hours.

Fry the onions, garlic, and ginger with extra virgin olive oil in a pan until golden brown.

Add the string beans and the mushrooms to the pan and add 3 tablespoons of tomato paste. Fry on medium heat for 20 minutes.

Add 2 pounds of fresh blended tomatoes (best done using a food processor).

Cover with a lid and cook for 20 minutes on medium heat.

Add 2 teaspoons of cinnamon and stir frequently.

Strain the rice and place it in a large pot with 6 cups of water. Bring to a boil on high heat for 20 minutes or until soft, and then strain the rice.

Add 5 tablespoons of extra virgin olive oil to a large pot. Layer the cooked rice and string bean mixture in 1-inch increments, alternating between the rice and the string bean mix.

Grind a pinch of saffron in a spice grinder and then mix it in a cup of hot water. Gently sprinkle the mixture onto the rice.

Put the pot on high heat for about 15 minutes, then switch to medium heat. Keep the lid on for 45 minutes.

Serve and enjoy!

Khoreshteh Karafs

SERVES 6 | PREP TIME 60 MIN

This celery & herb dish is filled with so many health benefits, substituting Portobello mushrooms (which are high in protein) for meat transforms this dish into a mouth-watering superfood stew.

Items you need

1 large white onion, minced

4 garlic cloves, minced

1 tbsp of turmeric

1 tbsp of freshly chopped ginger

1 bunch of parsley

1/2 bunch of mint

1/2 cup of extra virgin olive oil

1 bunch of celery

1 fresh lemon

2 large portobello mushrooms

1 lemon

1 bunch of green onion

Directions

Mince the onions, garlic, parsley, mint, ginger, and green onion.

Chop celery and mushrooms into small pieces.

Add 1 tablespoon of extra virgin olive oil into a frying pan, and sauté the onions, garlic, and ginger until golden brown.

Add celery and all spices to the pan.

Sauté on medium heat for 10 minutes.

Add in parsley, mint, green onions, portobello mushrooms, and sauté for another 15 minutes on medium-high heat.

Squeeze full lemon into the mixture and add 1/2 cup of water.

Cover with a lid and cook on medium for 45 minutes, stirring every 10 minutes.

Serve and enjoy!

Ghormeh Sabzi

SERVES 6 | PREP TIME OVERNIGHT

With a sophisticated selection of herbs, if there was a royal dish, this would be it! Traditionally made with meat, but we have refined it using Portobello mushrooms once again, adding more nutrients.

Items you need

1 large white onion, minced

4 garlic cloves, minced

1 tsp of freshly chopped ginger

2 bunches of fresh chopped parsley

1 bunch of fresh chopped coriander

3 bunches of green onions chopped

1/2 a bunch of fresh fenugreek leaf (can substitute the dry leaf if fresh is difficult to find)

1/2 cup of extra virgin olive oil

3 fresh limes, cut in half

1 small jalapeño, minced

2 cups of dried kidney beans

Salt and pepper to taste

Directions

Soak kidney beans in water overnight.

In a frying pan, add 2 tablespoons of extra virgin olive oil and sauté the garlic, onion, ginger, green onions, and spices for 10-15 minutes or until golden brown. Set mixture aside.

In a frying pan, add 2 tablespoons of extra virgin olive oil and sauté all the herbs until soft and the color has darkened.

Drain the kidney beans that have been soaking overnight.

In a large saucepan, mix the kidney beans, all the herbs, the jalapeño, garlic, and onion mixture with 2 cups of water. Squeeze limes into the mixture.

Cook on medium to low heat for 1 hour and 30 minutes, stirring every 10 minutes.

Serve and enjoy!

Agheh ReshTeh

SERVES 6 | PREP TIME OVERNIGHT

This is the perfect dish to make when you're experiencing childhood nostalgia or craving something comforting, at least it is for me!

Items you need

3 large white onions, minced

4 garlic cloves, minced

1 tsp of freshly chopped ginger

1 tbsp of organic ground turmeric

1/2 lb of Isfahani reshteh (will need to purchase from an Iranian specialty grocery)

3 bunches of green onions, chopped

1 bunch of parsley, minced

1 bunch of coriander, minced

1 bunch of dill, minced

1 bunch of fresh spinach

1 cup of dried chickpeas

1 cup of dried kidney beans

1 cup of dried green lentils

Salt and pepper to taste

1 small jalapeno

Directions

Soak the kidney beans, chickpeas, and lentils in water overnight.

Finely chop all the herbs, garlic, onions, ginger, jalapeños, and green onions.

In a frying pan, add 2 tablespoons of extra virgin olive oil and sauté the garlic, onion, ginger, green onions, and all of the spices for 10 to 15 minutes or until golden brown. Set mixture aside.

In a frying pan, add 2 tablespoons of extra virgin olive oil and sauté all the herbs until soft and the color has darkened.

Cook the lentils, chickpeas, and kidney beans separately. Boil with water and a little bit of salt and pepper to taste.

Serve and enjoy!

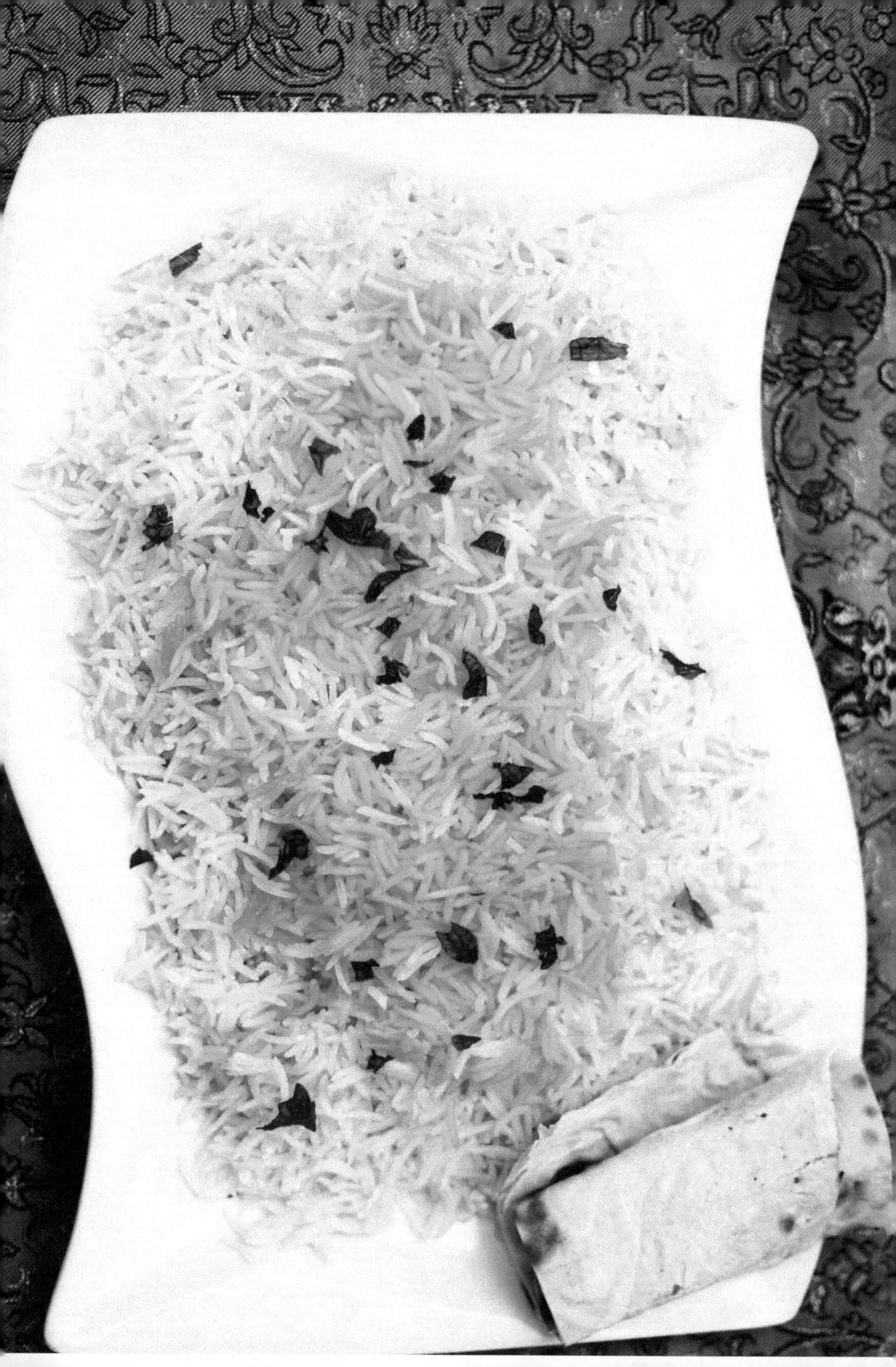

Persian Rice

SERVES 6 | PREP TIME 4HRS

Persian Rice is a dish that sounds complicated, but it is the furthest thing from complicated, just fancy! This dish will always be on the table during a Persian meal.

Items you need

6 cups of water

4 cups of basmati rice

4 tbsps salt

1 pinch of saffron

A handful of steamed

barberries

1 tbsps of chopped pistachios

Directions

Wash the rice 2 to 3 times. Then soak in water with 4 tablespoons of salt for 3 hours. Drain the rice into a large strainer.

Grind the saffron in a spice grinder.

Boil 1 cup of water and mix it with the saffron. Set aside.

In a large pot, add the rice and 6 cups of water with 1 teaspoon of salt. Bring to a boil and cook for 15 to 20 minutes or until the rice is slightly softened.

Take off of heat and drain the rice into a strainer.

In a large rice pot, add 4 tablespoons of extra virgin olive oil.

Add a 1-inch layer of rice and drizzle 1/4 cup of saffron water on top of the rice.

Slowly and gently layer the rice. Cook on high heat for 10 minutes. Cover with lid and cook on medium-low heat for 45 minutes.

Garnish with barberries and pistachios. Serve and enjoy!

Lavaghak

SERVES 1 (not to be shared) | PREP TIME

This is the perfect snack when you're craving something sweet and sour because it is made with clean and all-natural ingredients, so you can enjoy as much as you want, guilt-free.

Items you need

6 plums

1 1/2 cups of water

Parchment paper

Baking sheet Sunlight

Directions

Wash the plums, then place them in 1 and 1/2 cups of water. Boil until all of the water has evaporated.

Place plums in a strainer with large holes and push the mixture through holes, straining out the seeds. Toss seeds or plant them in your garden (for future Lavashaks).

Pour the plum mixture evenly onto the baking sheet.

Cover the baking sheet with parchment paper. Leave in direct sunlight for 2-3 days, or until completely dry.

Morabayeh Hafeej

SERVES 6-8 | PREP TIME 3 HOURS

This dish is both sweet and savory and can be eaten on toast for breakfast or alongside dinner, but I bet you'll find yourself enjoying it on its own too.

Items you need

5 large carrots, grated

1/2 cup of chopped almonds

2 tbsps of cardamon seeds

3 tbsps of dried orange peel

1 1/2 cups of water

500 grams of sugar

1 1/2 cups of water

1 tsp of vanilla extract

1 cup of shelled pistachios

1 fresh lime but in half

Directions

Soak almonds for 2 hours.

Boil orange peels in 2 cups of water.

Add carrots, sugar, cardamom seeds, vanilla extract, almonds, and 1 1/2 cups of water to a saucepan. Cook on medium heat, stirring every 5 minutes.

After 20 minutes, squeeze in half a fresh lime and add freshly chopped pistachios.

Continue to cook on medium heat for 20 minutes and add 5 teaspoons of pistachios just before plating.

Serve and enjoy!

THE PERSIAN VEGAN

COOKBOOK

Lightning Source UK Ltd.
Milton Keynes UK
UKHW050606260123
415933UK00014B/20

9 781088 036303